HILLSIDE PUBLIC LIBRARY

3 1992 00143 3227

W9-BFW-633

AUG 2 1 2003

HILLSIDE PUBLIC LIBRARY
405 N. HILLSIDE AVENUE
HILLSIDE, IL 60162
(708) 449-7510

DEMCO

Mountain Bikes

By Jeff Savage

Consultant:

Brian Fiske
Mountain Bike Magazine

CAPSTONE
HIGH-INTEREST
BOOKS

an imprint of Capstone Press
Mankato, Minnesota

HILLSIDE PUBLIC LIBRARY

Capstone High-Interest Books are published by Capstone Press
151 Good Counsel Drive, P.O. Box 669, Mankato, Minnesota 56002
http://www.capstone-press.com

Copyright © 2003 by Capstone Press. All rights reserved.
No part of this publication may be reproduced in whole or in part, or stored in a retrieval
system, or transmitted in any form or by any means, electronic, mechanical,
photocopying, recording, or otherwise, without written permission of the publisher.
For information regarding permission, write to Capstone Press,
151 Good Counsel Drive, P.O. Box 669, Dept. R, Mankato, Minnesota 56002.
Printed in the United States of America.

Library of Congress Cataloging-in-Publication Data
Savage, Jeff, 1961–
    Mountain bikes/by Jeff Savage.
    p. cm.—(Wild rides!)
    Summary: Provides an overview of the history and development of
mountain bicycles, their main features, and mountain bike competitions.
    Includes bibliographical references and index.
    ISBN 0-7368-1518-X (hardcover)
    1. All terrain bicycles—Juvenile literature. [1. All terrain bicycles. 2. All
terrain cycling.] I. Title. II. Series.
TL437.5.A43 S28 2003
796.6'3—dc21   2002012651

Editorial Credits
Matt Doeden, editor; Karen Risch, product planning editor; Kia Adams,
    series designer; Gene Bentdahl and Molly Nei, book designers;
    Jo Miller, photo researcher

Photo Credits
Corbis/Duomo, 14; Reuters NewsMedia Inc., 22, 28; Ales Fevzer, 24–25;
    AFP/Andree-Noelle Pot, 26
Getty Images/Mike Powell, 8–9
Photo by Ted Carlson/Fotodynamics, 18, 20
Photri-Microstock, 16
The Viesti Collection, Inc./Kevin Vandivier, cover; Thomas Kanzler, 7;
    Don Peha, 12
Visuals Unlimited/Steve Callahan, 4, 10

The author wishes to dedicate this book to Finley Gibbs—expert racer.

1 2 3 4 5 6 08 07 06 05 04 03

Table of Contents

Learn about:

BMX bikes and mountain bikes

Cost of mountain bikes

Off-road races

CHAPTER 1

Mountain Bikes

Fifty mountain bike racers gather at the starting line of a dirt racecourse. A woman fires a gun into the air to signal the beginning of the race. The riders stand and pedal as hard as they can into the course's first turn.

The riders remain in a tight group as they approach a steep hill. They shift into higher gears to make pedaling easier. They stand again and press down hard on the pedals to climb the hill.

The mountain bikes quickly gain speed as they coast down the other side of the hill. The riders tuck in their bodies. They keep their heads low to prevent air resistance from slowing the bikes. They quickly reach speeds of more than 25 miles (40 kilometers) per hour.

Several riders pull ahead of the pack. They slide around a sharp turn in single file. Dirt flies up from their tires. The riders bounce over rough bumps and grooves in the ground. As they splash through a creek, they hold their feet up to keep them out of the water. Finally, the riders make another turn and pedal toward their starting point. They have completed one 4-mile (6.4-kilometer) lap of the race. But they do not stop. They have four more laps to finish.

About Mountain Bikes

Mountain bikes are durable bicycles that can travel on almost any kind of surface. They handle well on dirt, rock, and pavement. Mountain bikers often ride on off-road trails that include many surfaces.

Mountain bikes combine the speed of standard road race bicycles with the durability of bicycle motocross (BMX) bikes. They have gear systems much like those of road race bicycles. But they are built with strong frames and wide tires like BMX bikes.

Inexpensive mountain bikes can cost $100 or less, but most mountain bikes cost more than $300. Professional racers may spend $5,000 or more on a new bike. They may spend thousands of dollars more to change their bikes to fit their needs.

Mountain bikes handle well on almost any surface.

Mountain Bikes in Action

Most mountain bikers ride on off-road trails. Many state parks and national parks have trails designed for mountain bikers. Riders can complete some trails in less than an hour. Longer trails may take a day or more to finish.

Some riders compete in mountain bike races. Cross-country races are among the most popular. These off-road races often include steep hills and sharp turns.

Downhill racing is also popular. Downhill races begin at the top of a steep hill. Riders race

one at a time down the hill. The rider with the fastest time wins the race.

Some highly skilled riders race professionally. They compete against other professional racers for cash prizes. They also may earn money through endorsements. Riders endorse products by wearing company logos or by using a company's equipment. They also may appear in advertisements for the company. Some professional riders earn enough in prize money and endorsements to make a living.

Cross-country races often include hills and sharp turns.

Learn about:

Clunkers

Growth in popularity

Mountain biking organizations

CHAPTER 2

Early Models of Mountain Bikes

The first modern mountain bikes were built in the 1970s. Some people give Gary Fisher credit for building one of the first models. He and his friends modified old Schwinn bikes to race down Mount Tamalpais in California. People in the area wanted bikes like his, so Fisher and his friends modified more bikes. They added gears to the bikes and gave them wider tires and stronger brakes. They often used parts from old bikes. People called the rebuilt bikes "clunkers." They later began calling them "mountain bikes."

BMX bikes were also popular during the 1970s. Riders often raced these small, off-road bikes on dirt courses. Mountain bikes looked somewhat like large BMX bikes. Some mountain bikers watched BMX races. They held similar races with their mountain bikes.

Mountain bike riders sometimes race on BMX-style racecourses.

Changes to the Sport

Soon, many North American riders began building their own mountain bikes. Like Fisher, they modified old bikes. They tried different designs. Most designs included strong, durable frames. Some riders added shock absorbers to give a smoother ride.

Mountain bikes continued to change. Major bike manufacturers began making mountain bikes. As mountain bike racing continued to grow, the companies built lighter and stronger bikes.

In 1983, a group of bikers formed the National Off-Road Bicycle Association (NORBA). This group organized many mountain bike races. It also helped set rules for the sport. NORBA remains an important organization in mountain biking today.

In 1988, the International Mountain Bicycling Association (IMBA) formed. This organization helped to create rules for off-road riders. The group encourages riders around the world to ride safely and responsibly.

Learn about:

Shock absorbers

Gear systems

Rims, tires, and brakes

CHAPTER 3

Designing a Mountain Bike

Today, manufacturers build many models of mountain bikes. The two main types are cross-country bikes and downhill bikes. Cross-country bikes are lightweight and easy to control. They can travel over almost any kind of surface. Downhill bikes are built to be durable and safe for downhill rides and races.

Riders often modify their bikes to fit their needs. They may adjust the handlebars and seat. They may add or remove shock absorbers in the suspension system to change the smoothness of the ride. Riders sometimes let air out of their tires to improve the tires' grip on the ground.

Top Tube

Seat Tube

Down Tube

Three strong tubes form a mountain bike's main triangle.

Frame

The frame is the body of a mountain bike. All of the bike's other parts connect to the frame. The main part of the frame is made of three tubes that join to form a triangle. The top tube stretches from the seat to the handlebars. The down tube connects with the top tube under the handlebars. The down tube extends to the area where the pedals are attached. There, the seat tube connects to the down tube. The seat tube connects to the top tube under the seat.

The frame also includes tubes that hold the wheels. Two tubes extend down from the front of the down tube. These tubes form the front fork and hold the front wheel. Four tubes hold the back wheel in place. They form the rear triangle.

Most downhill bike frames are made of a mixture of metals called an alloy. Most of these alloys include the metal aluminum. Some cross-country bikes have carbon fiber frames. Carbon fiber is a strong, lightweight material also used to build parts for fighter jet airplanes.

Springs called shock absorbers help give riders a smooth ride.

Suspension System

Mountain bikes have suspension systems to absorb much of the impact of bumps. Suspension systems include shock absorbers. These springs help prevent damage to the bike's frame. They also give the rider a much smoother ride and better control of the bike on rough ground.

Most downhill bikes have a shock absorber connected to each wheel. This setup is called full suspension. Most cross-country bikes have a shock absorber only on the front wheel. A bike with this setup is called a hardtail. Some cross-country bikes have no shock absorbers. These bikes are called rigid bikes. Some riders prefer rigid bikes because they are lightweight. But most mountain bikes come with suspension systems to give the riders better control over rough ground.

Drivetrain and Gears

A rider powers a mountain bike with the drivetrain, which includes the bike's pedals and gear system. The pedals are connected to metal arms called cranks. The cranks are attached to the bike's three front sprockets. A chain connects these small metal wheels to nine rear sprockets called cogs. The cogs turn as the rider pedals. This motion causes the back wheel to turn.

The rider shifts gears with levers attached to the handlebars. The chain shifts from one sprocket to another as the rider shifts gears. Most mountain bikes have 27 gears.

Calipers squeeze rubber pads against wheel rims to stop the wheels from turning.

Rims and Brakes

Mountain bike wheel rims are slightly smaller than the rims on road race bicycles. They usually measure 26 inches (66 centimeters) from top to bottom.

Mountain bike tires fit over the rims. The tires are usually at least 2 inches (5 centimeters) wide. They are more than twice as wide as the tires on road race bicycles. This width makes the bikes much more stable on uneven surfaces. Mountain bike tires include patterns of bumps and grooves called tread. Tread helps the tires grip uneven surfaces such as dirt. This grip is called traction.

Riders control the brakes with levers attached to the handlebars. Each brake is connected to a wheel rim. The rider's left hand controls the front brake. The right hand controls the rear brake.

Cables connect the brake levers to clamps called calipers. Calipers squeeze rubber pads against the wheel rims to slow down the bike. Some brake systems slow down the wheel at the center. They squeeze a piece of metal called a rotor that is attached to the wheel. These brakes are called disc brakes.

Learn about:

Popular events

Racing classes

Types of races

CHAPTER 4

Mountain Bikes in Competition

Riders of all ages and ability levels can compete in mountain bike competitions. NORBA holds races for both professional and amateur riders. Professional racers may compete in the NORBA National Championship Series and the World Cup Series held by the International Cycling Union.

Amateur riders are divided into classes according to their age and ability. The amateur classes include Beginner, Sport, Expert, and Semi-Pro. Men and women compete in separate classes. Some beginning riders compete in the American Mountain Bike Challenge. This series of 24 races takes place across North America. Children can take part in the Junior Olympic Mountain Bike Series or the Shimano Youth Series.

Cross-Country

Cross-country races are the most common mountain bike races. They often take place on hiking trails or on courses built just for mountain biking. Courses often include dirt mounds, rocks, muddy areas, and streams.

Most cross-country races are 5 to 25 miles (8 to 40 kilometers) long. Races for beginners often are shorter. They can be as short as 1 mile

(1.6 kilometers). Some races are much longer. For example, the Leadville 100 in Colorado is 100 miles (161 kilometers) long.

Cross-country racers often buy bikes built just for cross-country races. The bikes usually have lightweight frames. Heavy frames would slow down riders as they pedaled up steep hills. Many riders prefer hardtail bikes because they are lighter than full-suspension bikes.

Hundreds of riders may take part in many cross-country races.

Downhill racers speed down a slope as fast as they can.

Downhill

Many downhill events take place on ski slopes during summer when the snow has melted. Some downhill events take place while snow is still on the ground.

Several types of downhill events are common. In slalom races, sets of poles called gates are placed in the ground. Racers must weave their bikes through each set of gates. The all-out sprint is a straight downhill race. Racers ride from the top of a mountain to the bottom. They must go through rocky sections and sharp turns and over natural jumps. Racers may reach speeds of 60 miles (97 kilometers) per hour or more in these raccs. Only highly experienced riders should attempt this kind of riding.

Downhill bikes are usually heavier than cross-country bikes. Most downhill racers prefer full-suspension bikes. This setup softens the impact of the bumps as the bike speeds down a hill. Racers sometimes use extra-wide tires to improve traction and control.

Alison Dunlap

Alison Dunlap is one of the most famous mountain bike racers in the world. Dunlap was born July 27, 1969, in Denver, Colorado. She began racing bikes in 1988 and quickly became one of the world's best racers.

Dunlap won her first mountain bike race in 1995 in Japan. From 1997 to 1999, she won many major competitions, including the NORBA National Championship Series and the Pan American Games. USA Cycling named her Elite Mountain Bike Female Athlete of the Year for all three years. Dunlap finished seventh in the 2000 Olympic Games. She won the 2001 World Championships.

Dunlap has been in several serious crashes during her career. Her injuries have included a separated shoulder, three broken teeth, and a concussion. But she does not let the injuries stop her from enjoying her sport.

Words to Know

alloy (AL-oi)—a mixture of two or more metals

aluminum (uh-LOO-mi-nuhm)—a lightweight, silver-colored metal

axle (AK-suhl)—a rod in the center of a wheel around which the wheel turns

calipers (KAL-uh-purz)—a set of clamps at the end of a brake cable that press against a wheel's rim to stop the wheel from turning

drivetrain (DRIVE-trane)—the part of a vehicle that provides power to the axles

frame (FRAYM)—the body or tubing of a mountain bike

slalom (SLAH-luhm)—a type of race in which competitors must weave through sets of gates

sprocket (SPROK-it)—a wheel with a rim made of toothlike points that fit into the holes of a bicycle chain

traction (TRAK-shuhn)—the gripping power that holds a mountain bike's tires to the ground

tread (TRED)—a series of bumps and deep grooves on a tire; tread helps tires grip surfaces.

To Learn More

Hayhurst, Chris. *Mountain Biking!: Get on the Trail.* The Extreme Sports Collection. New York: Rosen, 2000.

Mason, Paul. *Mountain Biking.* To the Limit. Austin, Texas: Raintree Steck-Vaughn, 2001.

Molzahn, Arlene Bourgeois. *Extreme Mountain Biking.* Extreme Sports. Mankato, Minn.: Capstone Press, 2000.

Useful Addresses

Mountain Bike Magazine
33 East Minor Street
Emmaus, PA 18098

National Bicycle League
3958 Brown Park Drive
Suite D
Hilliard, OH 43026

USA Cycling
One Olympic Plaza
Colorado Springs, CO 80909

Internet Sites

Track down many sites about Mountain Bikes.
Visit the FACT HOUND at *http://www.facthound.com*

IT IS EASY! IT IS FUN!

1) Go to *http://www.facthound.com*
2) Type in: 073681518X
3) Click on "FETCH IT" and FACT HOUND will find
   several links hand-picked by our editors.

Relax and let our pal FACT HOUND do the research for you!

Index